The Situation
Is Hopeless,
But Not Serious

BY PAUL WATZLAWICK

W·W·NORTON & COMPANY
· New York · London

The Situation
Is Hopeless,
But Not Serious

[THE PURSUIT OF UNHAPPINESS]

Printed in the United States of America.

The text of this book is composed in 11/13 Palatino, with display
type set in Bauer Bodoni. Composition and manufacturing by The
Maple-Vail Book Manufacturing Group. Book Design by Nancy
Dale Muldoon.

The excerpt from *The Balcony* by Jean Genet (translated by Bernard
Frechtman) is reprinted with kind permission of the publisher.
© Grove Press, New York, 1966.

Library of Congress Cataloging in Publication Data

Watzlawick, Paul.
   The situation is hopeless, but not serious.
   Bibliography: p.
   1. Happiness—Anecdotes, facetiae, satire, etc.
   2. Psychology, Pathological—Anecdotes, facetiae,
   satire, etc.   I. Title.
   BF575.H27W37   1983   158'.1   83–8133

ISBN 0-393-01821-0

W. W. Norton & Company, Inc.,
500 Fifth Avenue, New York, N.Y. 10110
W. W. Norton & Company Ltd.,
10 Coptic Street, London WC1A 1PU

Contents

Contents

*I*N the heart of Europe there was once a great empire. It was composed of so many and so widely different cultures that no commonsense solution to any problem could ever be reached, and absurdity became the only possible way of life. Its inhabitants—the Austro-Hungarians, as the reader may already have suspected—thus were proverbial not only for their inability to cope reasonably with the simplest problems, but also for their ability to achieve the impossible somehow almost by default. Britain, as one bon mot claimed, loses every battle except the decisive ones; Austria loses every battle except the hopeless ones. (Small wonder, since the highest military decoration was reserved for officers who snatched victory from the jaws of defeat by taking some action that was in flat contradiction to the general battle plan.)

The great empire is now a tiny country, but absurdity has remained its inhabitants' outlook on life, and the author of these pages is no exception. For all of them, life is hopeless, but not serious.

Introduction

WHAT are we to expect from man . . . ? You may heap upon him every earthly blessing, you may submerge him in well-being until the bubbles shoot to the surface of his prosperity as though it were a pond, you may give him such economic success that nothing will be left for him to do but to sleep and to eat dainties and to prate about the continuity of the world's history; yes, you may do all this, but none the less, out of sheer ingratitude, sheer devilment, he will end by playing you some dirty trick. He will imperil his comfort, and purposely desiderate for himself deleterious rubbish, some improvident trash, for the sole purpose that he may alloy all the solemn good sense that has been lavished upon him with a portion of the futile, fantastical element which forms part of his very composition. Yet, it is these same fantastical dreams, this same debased stupidity, that he most wishes to retain. . . .

These words were written by the man whom Friedrich Nietzsche considered the greatest of all psychologists: Fyodor Mihailovich Dostoyevsky. And yet what they imply has been known since time immemorial—namely, that man is ill prepared to put up with sheer bliss.

It is about time to lay to rest the old wives' tale that luck, happiness, and contentment are desirable states of existence. For too long we have been told—and trustingly believed—that the search for happiness will eventually lead us to happiness.

The notion is particularly absurd when we realize that the word *happiness* cannot even be defined. "What happiness consists in has always been debated," writes the philosopher Robert Spaemann in an essay on the happy life. "Terentius Varro and, following him, Augustin counted 289 views of happiness. All humans want to be happy." And then Spaemann mentions the wisdom of the Jewish joke about the son who tells his father that he wants to marry Miss Katz. The father objects, Miss Katz has no dowry. The son insists that only with Miss Katz will he be happy. Thereupon the father says, "To

be happy—and what good will that do you?"
[23]*

A casual review of world literature alone
should make us suspicious. Disaster, tragedy,
catastrophe, crime, sin, madness, danger—that's
the stuff of all great literary creations. Dante's
Inferno is vastly more ingenious than his *Para-
diso;* the same goes for Milton's *Paradise Re-
gained,* which, when compared to *Paradise Lost,*
is rather insipid; *Faust I* moves us to tears,
Faust II to yawns.

Let's not fool ourselves: What or where
would we be without our unhappiness? We
badly need it, in the truest sense of the word
badly.

Our warm-blooded cousins in the animal
kingdom are no better off than we: Just look at
the monstrous effects of sheltering these splen-
did creatures in zoos, where they are protected
from hunger, danger, and illness (including
tooth decay). As a result, we turn them into the
animal equivalents of neurotics and psychotics.

Our world, drowning as it is in a tidal wave
of "how to" instructions for the attainment of
happiness, must no longer be deprived of a life-
saver for those in pursuit of unhappiness. No
longer must the knowledge of misery-producing
mechanisms and processes remain the jeal-

*Bracketed numbers refer to the Bibliography.

ously guarded secret of psychiatry and psychology.

The number of persons talented enough to create their own hell may seem relatively large. But many more are in need of help and encouragement. This little book is dedicated to them as an introductory text and guideline.

My endeavor is more than altruistic, however—it also has political and economic significance. For what the zoo directors practice on a small scale, modern governments try to achieve on a nationwide level, namely, to render their citizens' lives secure and dripping with happiness from cradle to grave. The road toward this noble goal requires, among other things, systematic and relentless education of citizens in the direction of greater and greater social incompetence. Small wonder, then, that increasingly astronomical amounts are spent throughout the world on health care and numerous other social projects.

To give a few examples: The total national health expenditures in the United States rose from $12.7 billion in 1950 to $247.2 billion in 1980, and the expenditures for drugs and medical sundries alone from $3.7 billion to $19.2 billion during the same period. The total social welfare expenditures show a similar vertiginous rise, from $23.5 billion in 1950 to $428.4 billion in 1979 [24]. Present West German statistics—to give just one European example—show that the *daily* expenditures of the health care system amount to 450 million German marks, that is, thirty times the amount spent in 1950; that there are at any given moment 10 million sick people in the German Federal Republic, and that the average West German swallows 30,000 pills in the course of his life.

Now imagine what would become of us if this trend were to level out or—God forbid—begin to reverse itself. Entire ministries and other monster bureaucracies would collapse, entire branches of industry would go bankrupt, and millions of people would be out of work.

To help avert this disaster, this book wishes to make a small but conscientious contribution. The modern state is in such dire need of the ever-increasing helplessness and unhappiness of its citizenry that the fulfillment of this need cannot be left to the well-intentioned but inept attempts of its individual citizens. As in all other walks of human life, here, too, government planning and direction is the road to success. Anybody can *be* unhappy, but to *make* oneself unhappy needs to be learned, and to this end some experience with a few personal blows of fate simply won't do.

Useful and helpful information is rare and usually quite unintentional, even in the professional (i.e., psychiatric and psychological) literature. So far as I know, only a few of my colleagues have dared to broach this touchy subject. Praiseworthy exceptions are the Franco-Canadians Rodolphe and Luc Morisette with their *Petit manuel de guérilla matrimoniale* [12], Guglielmo Gulotta's *Commedie e drammi nel matrimonio* [6], Ronald Laing's *Knots* [9], and Mara Selvini's *Il Mago smagato* [22]. In the latter, the renowned psychiatrist shows how school systems *need* the school psychologist's failures in order to steer clear of any change and to continue doing more of the same. Then there are the books of my friend Dan Greenburg: *How to Be a Jewish Mother** [4] and *How to Make Yourself Miserable* [5], that important work acclaimed by the critics as "the frank report that has taught 100,000 people how to lead truly meaningless lives." And, last by by no means least, the three most important representatives of the British school must be mentioned: Stephen Potter with his *Complete Upmanship* studies [18]; Laurence Peter, the discoverer of the Peter Principle [16]; and J. Northcote Parkinson, the world-famous proponent of the law named after him [14,15].

What this book wants to offer, beyond these

*To avoid any misunderstanding, let me quote from the author's introductory remarks, in which he says that "you don't have to be either Jewish or a mother to be a Jewish mother. An Irish waitress or an Italian barber could also be a Jewish mother."

excellent studies, is a methodic, basic introduction—drawn from decades of clinical experience—into the most useful and reliable mechanisms for the pursuit of unhappiness. In spite of this claim, however, what follows must not be taken as an exhaustive and complete compendium, but merely a set of instructions and suggestions that will enable the more talented of my readers to develop their own style.

The Situation
Is Hopeless,
But Not Serious

Chapter One

This Above All:
To Thine Own Self Be True!

THIS pearl of wisdom derives from Polonius, the Lord Chamberlain in *Hamlet*. It is important for our subject (the pursuit of unhappiness), because by being true to his own self, Polonius managed to get mistaken for a rat and was stabbed in his hiding place behind an arras. Obviously, another pearl of wisdom, the one about the eavesdropper who hears no good of himself, was then unknown in the Kingdom of Denmark.

One might object that in this instance the

concept of making oneself miserable is taken to extremes, but we must grant Shakespeare some poetic license. The principle remains valid.

It is quite simple to live in conflict with the world and especially with our human environment, but to produce unhappiness all by ourselves, in the privacy of our own minds, is much more difficult, both to achieve and to perfect. We may blame our partner for being unloving, attribute nasty intentions to the boss, and hold the weather responsible for our tensions, but how do we manage to turn ourselves into our own worst enemies?

The approaches to misery are marked by signposts displaying words of popular wisdom. These markers have been established by so-called common sense, by timeless instinct, or whatever name we want to give this miraculous source of inspiration. Never mind that for every one of these adages another one in direct opposition can usually be found. Consider, "Distance makes the heart grow fonder" and, "Out of sight, out of mind," as just one example. We need only choose *one* and adopt it as a guideline, as the expression of One's Own Self, to arrive at the conviction that there is only one right view: one's own. And from this vantage point it quickly becomes evident that the world is out of joint.

This is also the place where we can begin to

separate the experts from the dilettantes. The latter manage, albeit occasionally, to shrug their shoulders and carry on with the dreary business of everyday life. But the person who remains true to his Own Self is unwilling to make such shabby compromises. Having to choose between the way the world *is* and the way he knows it *should be* (a fateful choice touched upon long ago in the Upanishads), he will undauntedly opt for the latter and indignantly reject the former. As the captain of his ship, which the rats have already abandoned, he heroically steers into the stormy night. Quite a pity, actually, that his repertory of adages does not contain one that was known to the Romans: *Ducunt fata volentem, nolentem trahunt*—fate leads the willing and it drags along the unwilling.

For unwilling this person is indeed, and in a very special way. For him, unwillingness and stubborn refusal eventually become an all-inclusive obsession. In his attempt to be true to his Own Self, he is enveloped by a spirit of negation, for not to negate would make him untrue to himself. The mere fact that other people may recommend something becomes the very reason for rejecting it—even if, seen objectively, that something would be to his advantage. (Maturity, as a colleague of mine has defined it, is the ability to do something even though your parents have recommended it.)

However, the *true* genius manages to go to the ultimate extreme and with heroic determination rejects even what *he himself* considers the best decision, that is, the voice of his own reason. Thus the snake not only bites its own tail but actually devours itself, and a state of unhappiness is created that is beyond comparison.

Of course, for my less gifted readers this state of misery remains a sublime if unattainable goal.

Chapter Two

Four Games with the Past

TIME allegedly heals all wounds. This may be so, but need not deter us. For it is perfectly possible to shield oneself against this effect of time and to make the past into a reliable source of unhappiness. To achieve this, four mechanisms have been recognized since the dawn of time.

1. THE GLORIFICATION OF THE PAST

With a little bit of talent, even a beginner can manage to see his past through a rosy filter that screens out everything but the good and beautiful. Only those underachievers who are incapable of performing this trick and thus are stuck with a down-to-earth view of the past will continue to see their adolescence (to say nothing of their childhood) as an unpleasant period of *Weltschmerz,* past regrets, and future fears, and will not long for a single day of those long years to return. The more gifted unhappiness candidates, on the other hand, should really have no difficulty in seeing their youth as a kind of Paradise Lost and in making it into an inexhaustible reservoir of nostalgic misery.

One's youth, of course, is only *one* example. Another would be the deep sorrow about the breakup of a romantic relationship. Resist the voices of reason, of your memories, and of your well-meaning friends who may try to remind you that the relationship was already beyond hope and that time and again you wondered how you could escape this hell. Refuse to believe that separation is by far the lesser evil. Rather, convince yourself for the *n*th time that this time an earnest, honest "new beginning" will have the desired success. (It won't.) Let yourself be guided by the following eminently logical consideration: If the *loss* of your beloved causes such infernal pain, how divinely blissful it will be to *find* him or her again!* Isolate yourself from all

---

*Like many authors in these enlightened days, I have long pondered how to comply with the chauvinistically non-

other people, stay home, preferably in the immediate vicinity of the telephone, in order to be prepared for the decisive call that will transfigure your life. However, should the waiting become intolerable, you can always rely on the tried-and-true recipe of establishing an identical relationship with a similar partner—no matter how different from the former partner this new person may at first appear.

2. MRS. LOT

The additional advantage of a deep involvement with the past is that it does not leave much time to face the present. Only by riveting one's attention on the past is it possible to prevent those occasional, involuntary changes of perspective—of 90 or even 180 degrees—that would reveal that the present not only offers the potential for more unhappiness but also of un-unhappiness, to say nothing of something that might be entirely new. And such glimpses away from the past could very easily affect the credibility of our pessimistic convictions. In this regard we

chauvinistic requirement of always referring to both sexes and at the same time avoid such awful combinations as he and / or she, he / she, s / he, her / him, and the like. I herewith give up and ask my readers to imagine that, wherever applicable, whenever they read *he*, it really means *he or she*.

can look with admiration to our Biblical precep-
tress, Mrs. Lot—you remember her, don't you?
(Genesis 19:17 and 26) The Lord said to Lot and
his family, Escape for thy life; look not behind
thee, neither stay thou in all the plain; escape to
the mountain, lest thou be consumed. . . . But
[Lot's] wife looked back from behind him, and
she became a pillar of salt. (In fairness to Mrs.
Lot, we may assume that what was going on in
Sodom and Gomorrah was far more exciting than
the prospect of life on a bald mountain. But she
managed to get neither the one nor the other.)

3. THE FATAL GLASS OF BEER

In the film *The Fatal Glass of Beer,* W. C.
Fields, one of the great pioneers of American
comic films, shows us the frightening, irreversible decline of a promising young man who
cannot resist the temptation of drinking his first
glass of beer. The moral index finger, raised in
warning (even though slightly shaking with
Fields' suppressed laughter) cannot be over-
looked: The deed is rash, repentance long. And
how long! Just think of another Biblical person-
age, Eve, and that little bit of apple. . . .

This concept of fatality has its inherent,
undeniable advantages. For a long time the
advantages have been hushed up, but in our age
of enlightenment they must no longer be con-

cealed. Repentance or no repentance, of much greater importance for our subject is the fact that the irreparable, irreversible consequences of that first glass of beer, if they do not excuse all further glasses, certainly determine them. In other words, all right, here I stand, burdened with guilt; I should have known better, but now it is too late. *Then* I sinned, but *now* I am the victim of my own sin.

Admittedly, this method of self-laceration is not ideal. Let us look for some refinements. What if I had no hand in the original event? What if nobody can blame me for having contributed to it? Then, no doubt, I am a pure, innocent victim. And then let somebody come and try to question my sacrificial status or even suggest I do something about my misery. What was inflicted upon me by God, the world, fate, nature, chromosomes and hormones, society, parents, relatives, the police, teachers, doctors, bosses, and especially by my friends is so grievous that the mere insinuation that I could perhaps do something about it adds insult to injury. And, besides, it is also unscientific. Any psychology textbook shows clearly that one's personality is determined by events in the past, especially those in early infancy. And even a child knows that what once happened can never be undone. Incidentally, herein lies the deadly seriousness (and length) of competent psychological treatment.* What would become of us if more and more people convinced themselves that the situation is hopeless, but not serious? Consider the warning example of Austria, whose actual (although officially unrecognized) national anthem is the *gemütliche* song, dating back to the time of the bubonic plague: "Oh du lieber Augustin, alles is' hin" (very freely translated, "My, oh my, good God, everything's gone to pot").

Sometimes, albeit rarely, an independent and unpredictable course of events may of itself compensate for past deprivations and frustrations by dropping into our laps the reward we so desperately sought. But the true expert in unhappiness is not rattled by this turn of events. The formula, "Now it's too late, now I don't want it any more," enables him to remain in the ivory tower of his indignation and to prevent the healing of past injuries by constant licking of the wounds.

But the ultimate perfection of this game—which, of course, requires even more talent—consists of making the past responsible even for *good* things and of holding the good things accountable for present misery. Unsurpassed in

---

*If the reader finds it difficult to appreciate this point, he should consult the literature on this subject, for example Lawrence S. Kubie [8].

this regard is the genius of a Venetian dock worker who, after the departure of the Hapsburgs from Venice, is reported to have said, "Cursed be the Austrians who taught us to eat three times a day!"

4. THE LOST KEY, OR "MORE OF THE SAME"

Under a streetlamp there stands a drunk who searches and searches. A policeman comes along, asks him what he is looking for, and the man answers, "My keys." Now they both search. After a while the policeman wants to know whether the man is sure that he lost his key here, and the latter answers, "No, not here, back there—but there it is much too dark."

Do you find this absurd? If so, then you, too, are looking in the wrong place. For the whole point is that such a search will yield nothing except more of the same.

This deceptively simple formula, *more of the same,* is one of the most effective recipes for disaster that has gradually evolved on our planet. In the course of hundreds of millions of years, it has led to the extinction of entire species. It is a game with the past that was known to our animal ancestors even before the sixth day of creation.

Contrary to Game No. 3, with its attribution of blame to forces beyond one's control, this fourth game consists in the stubborn and unyielding retention of adaptations and solutions that at one time may have been the most successful or even the only possible ones. This is bound to become a problem, because all situations tend to change over the course of time. Our game No. 4 has its starting point here. On the one hand, it is obvious that no organism can react to its environment in a random fashion, that is, in one way today and quite differently tomorrow. The vital necessity of adequate adaptation leads to the emergence of specific patterns of behavior whose purpose, ideally, is successful and painless survival. For reasons that are not yet sufficiently understood, men as well as animals tend to consider these optimal adaptations as final and thus valid forever. This naïve assumption blinds us to the fact that these patterns are bound to become more and more anachronistic. It also makes it impossible for us to see that a number of other possible, feasible, and perhaps even better solutions exist—and, presumably, have always existed. This double blindness has a double effect: First, it makes the chosen solution more and more useless and the overall situation thus increasingly hopeless; secondly, this increasing discomfort, coupled with the unshakable belief that there is only this *one* solution, leaves only *one* conclusion—that one must do *more of the same*. And by doing more of the same, one gets more of the same misery.

The importance of this mechanism is evident. Even beginners without special training can apply it with ease. Indeed, its use is so widespread that since Freud's time it has provided a comfortable livelihood for generations of specialists, although they do not call it the "more of the same" recipe, but prefer the scientific-sounding term *neurosis*.

Never mind the name; what matters is the effect. And the effect is guaranteed so long as the student stays with two simple rules: First, there is only one possible, permitted, reasonable, logical solution, and if this solution has not yet produced the desired effect, apply it more forcefully. Secondly, under no circumstances doubt the *assumption* that there is only one solution; only its *application* may be questioned and "refined."

Chapter Three

Russians and Americans

WHO, you will probably ask, would behave as absurdly as the man who has lost his key? He knows and, in fact, tells the policeman that what he is looking for is not where he is searching for it. Admittedly, it is more difficult to find something in the darkness (of the past) than in the bright light (of the present). But beyond this obvious fact, the joke does not prove a thing.

Ha ha! And why, do you think, is the man supposed to be drunk? Because in order to lead up to its punch line, the joke needs to imply in this cheap fashion that there is something wrong with the man, that he knows something and yet behaves as if he didn't.

Let us take a closer look at this *something.* The anthropologist Margaret Mead is the author of the conundrum, "What is the difference between an American and a Russian?" The American, she said, will *pretend* to have a headache in order to get out of an unpleasant social obligation; the Russian would have to *have* the headache. *Ex oriente lux* is all we can say with envy, for you will agree that the Russian solution is far better and more elegant. The American, to be sure, achieves his purpose, but he knows he is lying. The Russian remains in harmony with his conscience. Not knowing *how* he does it, he manages to create a valid excuse and he need not feel responsible for it. And this is possible because his right hand, so to speak, does not know what his left hand is doing.

In this highly specialized area of the right and left hand, every generation has its own great masters, although they often remain anonymous and only occasionally emerge into the public spotlight. In our time, for instance, we admiringly read of two such men whose talents shall be described briefly.

The first is a certain Bobby Joe Keesee who, according to the United Press, 29 April 1975 [7], is serving 20 years in prison for conspiracy in the (then) unsolved kidnap-murder of a U.S. Vice Consul in Mexico. When asked before sentencing if he had anything to tell the court, Keesee said, "There's nothing more I could say. I got involved in something I realize was wrong." The semantics of the second sentence are impressive. *I got involved* may imply either deliberate action or the idea of having been caught up in something without awareness. But in either case the crucial point is the subsequent use of *I realize* in the present tense, obviously meaning that Keesee *now* knows that he did something very wrong. In other words, at the time he committed the crime this did not occur to him.

In and of itself, this is not particularly remarkable. But the matter becomes interesting and instructive if we read on and learn that in 1962 Keesee deserted from the Army, stole a plane, and flew to Cuba. Upon his return to the United States, this escapade earned him two years in prison, although he insisted that he had acted as a CIA agent. The CIA denied any connection. In 1970 he managed to turn up among a group of hostages held by Palestinian guerrilleros in Amman, and in 1973, to everybody's surprise, he was among a group of POWs released by the North Vietnamese. The newspapers rather aptly refer to Keesee as a "soldier of misfortune." And the reader will agree that this life-style presupposes an unusual talent for getting into hot water.

Less adventuresome, but much more dependable, is the life-style of Mike Maryn, who, according to a newspaper report dated 28 August 1977 [11], was mugged 83 times in five years. He has no idea how or why this keeps happening to him, and this gives the story an almost somnambulistic touch. Maryn is neither a jeweler nor a money lender. The attacks take place at night and in plain daylight. His attackers are young boys, teenagers, able-bodied men, and several women. Even the police are puzzled and lamely explain that "he just happens to be in the wrong place at the wrong time."

All right, you may say, but this still does not explain *how* one gets oneself into predicaments of the Keesee or Maryn type. One second, please; I shall try to explain.

Chapter Four

The Story of the Hammer

A MAN wants to hang a picture. He has a nail, but no hammer. The neighbor has one and our man decides to borrow it. But then and there a doubt occurs to him: "What if the neighbor won't let me have it? Yesterday he barely nodded when I greeted him. Perhaps he was in a hurry. But perhaps he pretended to be in a hurry because he does not like me. And why would he not like me? I have always been nice to him; he obviously imagines something. If someone wanted to borrow one of my tools, I would of course give it to him. So why doesn't he want to lend me his hammer? How can one refuse such a simple request? People like him really poison one's life. He probably even imagines that I depend on him just because he has a hammer. I'll give him a piece of my mind!" And so our man storms over to the neighbor's apartment and rings the bell. The neighbor opens the door, but before he can even say, "Good morning," our man shouts, "And you can keep your damned hammer, you oaf!"

The effect of this technique is stunning, although the technique itself is quite simple and not very novel. Two thousand years ago, in his *Ars amandi*, Ovid described it, albeit only in positive terms: "Convince yourself that you love where you desire only fleetingly. Then believe it. . . . He loves rightly who succeeded in talking himself into passion."

If you can follow Ovid's advice, you should not find it difficult to use it in the service of achieving unhappiness. There are probably few mechanisms that can equal the effects of confronting an unsuspecting partner with the last link of a long, complicated chain of fantasies in which he plays a decisive, negative role. His bewilderment and confusion, his alleged incomprehension, his anger, his attempts to deny his guilt, all are conclusive proofs that you were right, that you had granted your favors to someone who did not deserve them, and that once again your kindness has been taken advantage of.

But as with any other technique, here, too, the expert may run into an even greater expert, and the moral of the hammer story is no exception. The sociologist Howard Higman of the University of Colorado is reported to have identified a particular communication that he calls the "nonspecific particular." According to one example, mentioned by Henry Fairlie in "My Favorite Sociologist" [2], wives tend to get their husbands to go from one room to another by shouting,

"What are these?" She expects the man to get up and go to see what she is talking about, and usually she is not disappointed. But one friend once struck back at his wife. . . . When his wife returned home one day, and shouted to him in his study, "Did they come?" the husband, not knowing what she was talking about, nevertheless said "Yes!" The wife shouted to him again. "Where did you put them?" He shouted back, "With the others." For the first time in years of matrimony, the rest of his day at work was undisturbed.

Let us go back to Ovid or, rather, to his successors. One who comes to mind above all others is the French pharmacist Emile Coué (1857–1926). He was the founder of a school of self-suggestion that was based on telling oneself relentlessly, "Every day in every way things are getting better and better." This, of course, runs contrary to the intent of this book, but even a mediocre talent should succeed in turning Coué

41

upside down in order to profit from his technique in the pursuit of unhappiness.

And with this, at long last, we are in a position to look at the practical applications of the foregoing. We have realized that the indispensable ability to not let the right hand know what the left is doing can be learned. To this end a series of exercises have been developed and will now be described.

EXERCISE 1

Sit down in a comfortable chair, preferably one with arm rests, close your eyes, and imagine that you are biting into a thick, juicy slice of lemon. With a little practice this imaginary lemon will actually make your mouth water.

EXERCISE 2

Remain seated in your chair, keep your eyes closed, and now shift your thoughts from the lemon to your shoes. It should not take you too long to realize, perhaps for the first time, how very uncomfortable it is to wear shoes. It does not matter how well they seemed to fit until this moment, because you will now become aware of pressure points and other unpleasant sensations, like friction, the bending of your toes, the tightness of the laces, heat or cold, and the like.

Repeat the exercise until the wearing of shoes, until now a simple and trivial necessity, becomes a decidedly uncomfortable problem. Buy a new pair and notice that no matter how perfectly they seemed to fit in the store, they will soon produce the same discomfort as the old ones.

EXERCISE 3

Still seated in your chair, look through the window into the sky. With a little bit of luck you will soon notice a large number of tiny, bubble-like circles in your visual field. When you keep your eyes fixed, the circles will gradually drift downward; when you blink, they jump up again. Notice further that these circles appear to grow in size and number as you concentrate on them. Consider the possibility of an insidious eye disease, for it is clear that your eyesight will be severely impaired once these circles finish covering your entire field of vision. Consult an ophthalmologist. He will try to explain to you that you are worrying about something that is perfectly harmless and normal, namely, what are called *floaters*. Now assume, please, that he was either in bed with the measles when this disease was taught to his class in medical school, or that out of sheer compassion he does not want to inform you of the incurable nature of your illness.

EXERCISE 4

Should you have difficulty with Exercise 3, there is no need for despair. Your ears offer an equivalent opportunity for worry. Go to a quiet room and you will soon notice a humming, buzzing, whistling, or similarly monotonous sound in your ears. In everyday situations this sound is drowned out by the noise around you, but with enough attention to it, you will hear it more and more often and it will become louder. Go to see your doctor. From this point on proceed in accordance with Exercise 3, except that the physician will try to minimize your symptom by calling it a perfectly normal *tinnitus*.

(Special instructions for medical students: You may skip Exercises 3 and 4, since you are already fully engaged in discovering within yourself the five thousand symptoms that alone form the basis of internal medicine, to say nothing of the other medical specialties.)

EXERCISE 5

You are now sufficiently trained and obviously talented enough to transfer your abilities from your body to the outside world. Let's begin with traffic lights. You may already have noticed that they tend to stay green until you come along, and then turn yellow and red pre-

cisely when it would be too risky to drive
through the intersection. If you succeed in
resisting the voice of reason that tells you that
on the whole you come up against as many green
as red lights, success is imminent. Without
knowing how you manage to do it, you will add
every successive red light to all the others that
have already forced you to stop, while the green
ones somehow will not register. Quite soon the
suspicion will solidify in your mind that you are
up against strange, hostile powers whose evil
machinations are by no means limited to your
hometown. Indeed, they have no difficulty following you to Los Angeles or Oslo.

If you do not drive yourself, you may utilize
the discovery that your line in front of the post
office window or bank teller is always the slow-
est, or that your plane always departs from the
gate that is most distant from the check-in
counter.

EXERCISE 6

You have now developed a growing awareness of the unusual and suspicious connections
between seemingly trivial and unrelated events.
It will enable you to detect remarkable and ominous links between facts that totally escape the
dull, routine world view of most people. Examine your front door carefully until you find a

scratch you never noticed before. Ask yourself what it may mean: Is it a so-called thief's mark or the result of an already attempted burglary, damage deliberately inflicted on your property by some unknown enemy or a special sign to identify your home for some sinister purpose? Again, resist the temptation to shrug off your concern. At the same time, do not make the mistake of trying to get to the bottom of the matter. Treat the problem in a purely abstract, intellectual fashion, for any reality testing would be detrimental to the effects of this exercise. (More about this danger in the next chapter.)

Once you have developed your own style and sharpened your eye for outlandish and mysterious connections, you will soon notice the unbelievable degree to which our everyday lives are interlaced with baffling, improbable coincidences. You will also begin to rely increasingly on your powers to detect these coincidences. A simple, prosaic example: You are waiting for the bus. To while away the time, you are reading a newspaper, but every once in a while you look down the street, hoping for the arrival of the bus. Suddenly your sixth sense tells you, "Here it comes!" You look, and sure enough, way down the street, still several blocks away, the bus has appeared. Remarkable, isn't it? And yet, this is only a small, neutral example of the many almost clairvoyant insights that are now crystallizing within you and which serve you best in the case of ominous, dangerous portents.

EXERCISE 7

As soon as you are sufficiently convinced that something suspicious is going on around you, discuss your impressions with your friends and acquaintances (if necessary, include the postman). There is no better way of separating your true friends from those wolves in sheep's clothing who are somehow involved in the conspiracy. For in spite of—or perhaps because of—their cleverness, they will give themselves away by trying to persuade you that there is nothing to your suspicions. This will not surprise you, for it goes without saying that whoever wants to hurt you surreptitiously will not openly admit it. Rather, that person will hypocritically attempt to distract you from your allegedly unfounded suspicions and convince you of his good, friendly intentions toward you. And with this you now not only know who is in on the conspiracy, but you know that there *has* to be something to the entire matter; otherwise, why would your "friends" try so hard to convince you of the contrary?

Readers who have conscientiously practiced these exercises will find that the skills described are not limited to Margaret Mead's Russian, the man with the hammer, or natural geniuses like Keesee and Maryn. Any average citizen can eventually arrive at the point where he can create a difficult situation and yet remain totally unaware of having done so. Helplessly exposed to powers beyond his control, he can suffer to his heart's content. A word of warning, however. . . .

Chapter Five

A Handful of Beans

THE attainment of such higher levels of consciousness is not as easy as the previous chapter may have made it appear. Failure cannot be excluded, and perhaps the most serious failure is documented in the following story.

On her death bed a young wife demands that her husband promise never to get involved with another woman. If he were to break his promise, she would return as a ghost and cause him endless trouble.

At first the man keeps his promise, but several months after the wife's death he meets another woman and falls in love. Soon thereafter a female ghost begins to appear every night and to accuse him of having broken his pledge. She not only knows everything that goes on between the man and his beloved, but also his innermost thoughts, hopes, and feelings. As the situation becomes unbearable, the man goes to see a Zen master and asks him for help.

Now this master knows his business. At least he seems to know that there is no point in trying to convince the man that there are no ghosts, that it is all in his head, and so forth. So, instead, he tells the man to wait for the ghost's next appearance and then, while praising her for being such a clever ghost, to take a handful of soybeans and ask her how many beans he has in his hand. If the ghost cannot answer this question, the man will know that she is a figment of his imagination and she will not bother him any more.

The following night when the ghost appears on schedule, the man begins to flatter her. "Indeed," says the ghost, "I do know everything. I even know that you went to see that Zen master." "And since you know so much," replies the man, "tell me how many beans I hold here in my hand."

There was no longer any ghost to answer the question [19].

You see, this is the complication that I had in mind earlier (in Exercise 6) when I warned that any reality testing is bound to lead to disappointing anticlimaxes. Therefore, should your despair and insomnia drive you to see the modern equivalent of a Zen master, you should at least consult one who is himself against such anticlimactic solutions. Go and see a descendant of Mrs. Lot, someone who is willing to play Game No. 2 with the past (see p. 27) with you by taking you on a virtually endless search, back to your earliest childhood and even farther back than that.

Chapter Six

Chasing Away the Elephants

THE last chapters were devoted to the development and gradual perfection of the ability to not let the right hand know what the left one is doing. We shall now proceed to another technique. Here the focus will not be on the creation of problems, but on the avoidance of problems for the purpose of their perpetuation.

The basic pattern is contained in the story of the man who claps his hands every ten seconds. When asked the reason for this strange behavior, he replies, "To chase away the elephants." "Elephants? But there aren't any around!" Whereupon the man says, "Right. See, I told you so!"

As the story shows, avoidance of a feared situation or problem does appear to be the simplest and most reasonable solution, but this solution also perpetuates the problem. For our purposes, the double effect of avoidance is especially useful. To make this point clear, let us look at another example: If a horse receives an electric shock in one of its hooves through a metal plate on the floor of its stall, and if a few seconds before the shock is administered a bell is rung, the animal rather quickly establishes a causal connection between the bell and the shock. From then on, every time the bell rings, the horse lifts its hoof—obviously to avoid receiving a shock. Once this association between the two events is established, the shock is no longer necessary and the bell alone invariably causes the horse to lift its leg. Every one of these acts of avoidance then seems to reinforce in the animal the "conviction" that it has successfully avoided the painful event. What the horse does not know and—thanks to its avoidance—*will never know,* is that the danger no longer exists.*

You see, what we are up against here is not a simple superstitition. Superstitious actions are

---

*Incidentally, the opposite of avoidance takes place in the romantic quest for the Blue Flower. While the avoidance perpetuates the problem, the belief in the (totally unproven) existence of the Blue Flower perpetuates the quest.

notoriously unreliable; but the effect of avoid-
ances is something every seeker of unhappiness
can confidently count on. And, moreover, the
practical application of this technique is much
simpler than it may at first seem. For essentially
it is no more than a consistent application of
common sense—and what could be more reasonable?

No one disagrees that many of our most
routine activities contain an element of danger.
How many dangers should we be willing to risk?
Reason and common sense suggest a minimum
or, if possible, none at all. Even the more daring
among us will consider professional boxing or
hang-gliding to be too risky. Driving? Think of
how many people are killed or maimed in traffic
accidents every day. But even walking entails
certain dangers that soon reveal themselves to
the searching view of reason. Pickpockets,
exhaust fumes, collapsing buildings, shoot-outs
between bank robbers and the police, incandes-
cent fragments of American or Soviet space sat-
ellites—the list of dangers is endless and only a
fool will blindly expose himself to these risks. It
is certainly safer to stay home. But even there
one's safety is relative. At home there are stairs,
the well-known assorted dangers of kitchens and
bathrooms, slippery floors or crumpled carpets,
knives, forks, to say nothing of gas, hot water,
and electricity. The only reasonable conclusion

would be to stay in bed. But what protection does the bed offer in the event of an earthquake? And what if one develops bed sores?

But I exaggerate. Only a few, truly gifted individuals will manage to become reasonable enough to anticipate and guard themselves against *all* imaginable dangers, including air pollution, contaminated drinking water, cholesterol, triglycerides, carcinogenic substances in food, and hundreds of other dangers and poisons.

The average citizen usually falls short of pushing his reason to this all-embracing view (and avoidance) of the totality of all imaginable and unimaginable dangers, and of thereby becoming entitled to 100% disability compensation. We lesser minds must content ourselves with partial successes. Let us not become perfectionists. Less ambitious goals may be quite satisfying, especially if they result from the concentrated application of reason and common sense to a minor problem. Knives can hurt; doorknobs are indeed covered with bacteria. Who knows, after all, that he will not have to go to the toilet in the middle of a symphony concert? Can anyone be sure he has not opened, rather than locked, the door when checking whether it was safely locked? A truly reasonable man therefore avoids sharp knives, touches doorknobs only with gloves, does not go to concerts, and convinces himself several times that the door is really locked. All of this is quite easy, except for the ever-present danger of gradually paying less and less attention to the problem and eventually losing sight of it. The following story illustrates how this danger can be avoided.

An elderly spinster who lives by the river complains to the police about a group of little boys bathing in the nude in front of her house. The constable dispatches one of his men, who tells the boys to move away. The next day the woman complains again: The boys are still within sight. The policeman goes back and sends them farther upstream. A day or so later the spinster quite indignantly calls again: "If I go up to the roof with a pair of field glasses, I can still see them."

We may now ask ourselves: What will the elderly spinster do when the little boys are definitely out of sight? Maybe she will go on long walks upstream, maybe she will be satisfied with the knowledge that *somewhere* some people are likely to be bathing in the nude. One thing is certain: The idea will continue to occupy her mind. And this is the *one* thing that matters.

The *other* is even more important. Any idea, when firmly held, nurtured, and cultivated, will eventually create its own reality. Let us next examine this eminently useful phenomenon.

Chapter Seven

Self-Fulfilling Prophecies

YOUR horoscope in today's paper warns you (and approximately 300 million other people born under the same sign) of the possibility of an accident. And sure enough, you slip and fall. So there is something to astrology after all.

Or is there? Are you sure that you would have slipped even if you had *not* read the prediction? Or if you were convinced that astrology is sheer nonsense? Unfortunately, these questions cannot be answered one way or the other after the fact.

The philosopher Karl Popper developed the interesting idea, here expressed in rather simplistic terms, that the very actions Oedipus took in order to *avoid* the horrifying predictions of the oracle led to the fatal fulfillment of those predictions.

Here, then, we are up against yet another effect of avoidance, namely, the possibility that under certain circumstances it may bring about precisely that which it was meant to prevent and avoid. And what are those circumstances? First, a prediction in the widest sense of the term, that is, any expectation, preoccupation, conviction, belief, or simply suspicion that things are going to take a certain course and not another. It does not seem to matter how these expectations are created—whether by beliefs or suggestions transmitted to us by other people, or by our own inner convictions. Second, the expectation thus created must not be seen as a simple possibility but, rather, as the reliable anticipation of an imminent event requiring immediate action for its avoidance. Third, this assumption will be all the more convincing if more people share it, less so if it contradicts common sense, social rules, or past experience.

For instance, it is enough to arrive at the conviction—no matter whether it is in some sense objectively justified or quite absurd—that others are whispering behind our backs and secretly ridiculing us. Faced with these "facts," our common sense will suggest that it would be foolish to trust these people. And since all of their actions take place under a rather flimsy veil of secrecy, it makes good sense to be on guard and pay attention to even the most minute details. It is then only a question of time until we do catch them in the act of whispering, secretly giggling, and exchanging conspiratorial winks and nods. The prophecy has fulfilled itself.

Success is guaranteed as long as you manage to remain unaware of your own contribution to this pattern. Happily, in the last chapters you have learned how to avoid just this. And once this form of interpersonal game has been going on for some time, it is no longer important (or even possible to verify) what came first: Your suspicious behavior that strikes the others as ridiculous or their behavior that makes you suspicious.

Self-fulfilling prophecies have a truly magical, "reality"-creating effect and are thus of the utmost importance for our subject. They have their established place not only in the repertory of any individual student of unhappiness, but also in the wider frame of society as a whole. For instance, history shows that if the members of a social or ethnic minority are consistently barred from certain forms of "honest" work (e.g., agriculture or trades) because the majority considers them to be dishonest, lazy, greedy, or above all "different from us," they will be forced to make their living as junk dealers, pawn brokers, smugglers, and the like. Of course, these people engage in these activities *because* they are social misfits, and it therefore makes sense to bar them from the activities of us good people. The more stop signs are put up by the city, the more drivers will become traffic violators whose reckless driving will necessitate additional stop signs. The more a nation feels threatened by its neighbor, the more it will arm itself, and the more the neighbor will be convinced of the need to take "defensive" measures. The outbreak of a war (which everybody has come to expect) is then only a question of time. The higher the taxes imposed in order to make up for (actual or supposed) tax evasions, the more otherwise honest citizens will tend to submit untrue tax declarations. Any prediction of an imminent shortage (whether correct or incorrect) of a given commodity, if believed by a sufficiently large number of people, will lead to the immediate hoarding of that commodity and thus to the predicted scarcity.

The prophecy of the event leads to the event of the prophecy. As mentioned above, the only precondition is that we convince ourselves, or let others convince us, of the imminence of something whose occurrence we consider to be quite independent of us.* And very much like Oedipus we thereby arrive exactly where we did not want to be. The experts, however, know how arriving can be avoided. This is our next consideration.

*Perhaps this is even the reason why spiritual seances or extrasensory perception experiments "must" fail if there is a disbeliever in the group.

Chapter Eight
Beware of Arriving

IT is better to travel hopefully than to arrive, says the wisdom of a Japanese proverb. But the Japanese are not the only ones who are leery of arriving. Lao Tzu recommended that we forget the task once it is accomplished. Shakespeare writes in his 129th sonnet,

> Enjoyed no sooner but despised straight,
> Past reason hunted, and no sooner had
> Past reason hated, as a swallowed bait
> On purpose laid to make the taker mad. . . .

And Oscar Wilde comes to mind with his famous and often plagiarized aphorism: There are two tragedies in life. One is not to get your heart's desire; the other is to get it.

Hermann Hesse's *Seductor* (in the poem of the same title) implores the personification of his desires: "Resist me, beautiful woman, tighten your robe! Enchant, torment me—but do not grant me your favors . . ."—knowing full well "that reality destroys the dream." Hermann Hesse's contemporary, Alfred Adler, struggled with the same problem much more concretely, if less poetically. Adler's work, whose rediscovery is more than overdue, deals extensively with the life-style of the eternal traveler who is careful not to arrive.

Greatly simplifying Adler's basic idea, the rules of this game with the future are the following: Arriving—by which is meant either literally or metaphorically reaching a destination—is generally taken to be an important criterion of success, power, recognition, and self-esteem. By the same token, failure or, especially, indolent drifting is considered a sign of stupidity, laziness, irresponsibility, or cowardice. But the road to success is troublesome, for it requires a great deal of effort and even the most intense effort may still fail. And who wants to go to this trouble? Thus instead of engaging in a "policy of small steps" toward a reasonable, reachable achievement, it is very useful to set oneself a goal that is admirably lofty. The advantages of this strategy should be immediately obvious to my readers. The Faustian striving for knowledge and mastery, the quest for the Blue Flower, the ascetic renunciation of life's lower satisfactions, all this carries a high degree of social approval (and your mother's admiration). And above all, if the goal is that high and distant, even the most stupid among us will understand that the road to that goal will be long and cumbersome, and that the travel will require extensive and time-consuming preparations. Therefore, who dares to blame us if we have not yet gotten started or if, once on our way, we get lost, march around in circles, or sit down for lengthy rests? If anything, history and literature are full of heroic examples of seekers who got lost in some labyrinth or tragically failed in the performance of some superhuman task, and who enable us lesser seekers to profit from their fateful glory.

Yet this is not the whole story. Even the arrival at the most sublime goal is fraught with a special danger, the common denominator of the quotations at the beginning of this chapter, namely, the disenchantment of successful arriving. The talented unhappiness expert knows of this danger, consciously or unconsciously. It would appear that the creator of our world has ordained the unattained goal to be so much more desirable, romantic and ecstatic than it turns out to be when we get there. Let's not fool ourselves: The honeymoon prematurely loses its sweetness; upon arrival in the distant, exotic city the taxi driver tries to cheat us; the successfully accomplished final examination creates little more than a host of additional, unexpected complications and responsibilities; and the alleged serenity of life after retirement is not half as ideal as it is made out to be.

Nonsense, the more sanguine types among us will say: Whoever is willing to settle for such mild, anemic ideals deserves to find himself empty-handed in the end. What, instead, of the passionate affect that exceeds itself in the climax of its gratification? Or the holy rage that leads to the intoxicating act of revenge for injuries suffered and to the restoration of universal justice? Who in the face of these gratifications could still speak of the "disenchantment" of arriving?

Unfortunately it does not quite seem to work out that way. And those who are not yet convinced should read what George Orwell has to say in his essay *Revenge Is Sour* [13]. True, it contains some considerations of such profound decency and conciliatory wisdom that they are actually out of place in a manual for the pursuit of unhappiness. But I hope my readers will forgive me for quoting them all the same, if only because they are so pertinent to our topic.

In 1945, in his capacity of war correspondent, Orwell visited a prisoner-of-war camp in

68

South Germany. He was shown around by a young Viennese Jew who was in charge of interrogations. As they came to a special section where high-ranking SS officers were detained, the young man delivered a fearful kick with his heavy army boot to the grotesquely swollen foot of one of the prisoners. The German officer had held a post corresponding to a general in the political branch of the SS.

It could be taken as quite certain that he had had charge of concentration camps and had presided over tortures and hangings. In short, he represented everything that we had been fighting against during the past five years. . . .

It is absurd to blame any German or Austrian Jew for getting his own back at the Nazis. Heaven knows what scores this particular man may have had to wipe out; very likely his whole family had been murdered; and, after all, even a wanton kick to a prisoner is a very tiny thing compared with the outrages committed by the Hitler régime. But what this scene, and much else that I saw in Germany, brought home to me was that the whole idea of revenge and punishment is a childish day-dream. Properly speaking, there is no such thing as revenge. Revenge is an act which you want to commit when you are powerless and because you are powerless: as soon as the sense of impotence is removed, the desire evaporates also.

Who would not have jumped for joy, in 1940, at the thought of seeing SS officers kicked and humiliated? But when the thing becomes possible, it is merely pathetic and disgusting.

And then, in the same essay, Orwell tells how a few hours after the fall of Stuttgart he and a Belgian war correspondent entered the city. The Belgian—and who could blame him?—was even more anti-German than the average Englishman or American.

We had to enter by a small footbridge which the Germans had evidently made efforts to defend. A dead German soldier was lying supine at the foot of the steps. His face was a waxy yellow. . . .
The Belgian averted his face as we went past. When we were well over the bridge he confided to me that this was the first time that he had seen a dead man. I suppose he was thirty-five years old, and for four years he had been doing war propaganda over the radio.

This *one* "arrival" becomes a decisive experience for the Belgian. It completely changes his attitude toward the "Boches":

When he left, he gave the residue of the coffee we had brought with us to the Germans on whom we were billeted. A week earlier he would probably have been scandalised at the idea of giving coffee to a "Boche." But his feelings, he told me, had undergone a change at the sight of *"ce pauvre mort"* beside the bridge: it had suddenly brought home to him the meaning of war. And yet, if we had happened to enter the town by another route, he might have been spared the experience of seeing even one corpse out of the—perhaps—twenty million that the war had produced.

But back to our real subject. If not even revenge is sweet, how much less sweetness is there in arriving at a supposedly happy goal? Therefore: Beware of arriving. (And, incidentally, why did Sir Thomas More call that distant island of happiness Utopia, that is, *Nowhere?*)

Chapter Nine

If You Really Loved Me, You Would Like Garlic

L'ENFER—*c'est les autres* (Hell—is other people) is a famous line from the last scene of Jean-Paul Sartre's play *No Exit*. If you, dear reader, have the impression that this subject has so far received too little attention, or none at all, that I have limited my helpful suggestions to the production of unhappiness all by yourself, in artificial isolation, you are right. The time has come to explore and familiarize ourselves with the baroque hell of human relationships, and to learn from the professional expertise of relationship demolition experts (referred to from now on as RDEs).

Let us try to approach the subject in a reasonably methodical fashion. About seventy years ago Bertrand Russell insisted on a strict separation between statements about things and statements about relations. "This apple is red" is a statement about the properties of *this* apple. But "This apple is bigger than that one" is a statement about the relationship *between* these two apples. It does not make sense if applied to one or the other apple separately, for the proposition "bigger than" is not located in one of them, but in their relation to each other.

This important distinction was later utilized and further developed by the anthropologist and communication researcher Gregory Bateson. He pointed out that both types of statements are always contained in every human communication, and he called them the *object* and the *relationship* level, respectively. This distinction helps us to understand more clearly how we can quickly get into trouble with a partner— any partner, but the closer the better. Let's assume that a wife says to her husband, "I made this soup from a new recipe. Do you like it?" If he likes it, he will have no problem saying yes and she will be happy. If he does not like the soup and if it does not bother him to disappoint her, he can simply say no. But a problem arises immediately if he finds the soup ghastly (a statistically much more probable case) but does not want to hurt her. On the *object* level (i.e., so far as the object *soup* is concerned), his answer would have to be no; but on the *relationship* level he would have to say yes, since he does not want to hurt her. But since we only have *one* language for both levels of discourse, what is the husband to say? His answer cannot be yes *and* no. In all probability he will try to wriggle out of this predicament by saying something like, "Tastes interesting," hoping that she will understand what he is really trying to tell her.*

His chances are minimal. Probably the best he can do under the circumstances is to emulate the example of a certain husband of my own acquaintance. At the very first breakfast after their wedding the wife placed a large box of corn flakes on the table, in the (on the object level) erroneous but (on the relationship level) well-meant assumption that the husband liked them. He did not want to hurt her and decided to eat

---

*Purists among the so-called "communication trainers" who ingenuously believe that there is such a thing as "correct" communication (whose grammar can be learned like that of a foreign language) probably have another answer, for instance, "I do not like the soup, but I sincerely want to thank you for having gone to the trouble of making it." Only in the books of these experts does the wife thereupon happily throw her arms around the husband's neck.

the awful stuff and then, when the box was empty, ask her not to buy more corn flakes. As a devoted wife, however, she had paid attention and just before he was finished with the first box, there stood the second. Now, sixteen years later, he has abandoned all hope of explaining gently that he hates corn flakes. One could imagine her reaction.

Or let us look at the seemingly harmless request, "Would you like to take me to the airport tomorrow morning?" Yes, yes, I know, the "correct" answer would have to be given separately on the two communication levels: for instance, "No, I very much dislike driving to the airport at six in the morning, but I am more than willing to do you that favor."

You may already have guessed how important this communication problem is for our subject. For even if the partner manages to express himself in the manner just described (and who, after all, talks in this stilted fashion?) the RDE can manufacture a problem out of the situation by a declaration of unwillingness to accept the favor unless the other *really likes* to drive to the airport. And no matter how the other now tries to wiggle out of this semantic trap, he will not escape the snares of the confusion between the object and relationship levels. At the end of the long, fruitless debate the partners will be very angry at each other. You see, the formula is relatively simple once you have grasped the crucial difference between these two levels of communication and are capable of confusing them not only inadvertently but deliberately.

All of this comes easy even for beginners because of the difficulty of making statements on the relationship level. One of the most edifying examples known to me is the confusion between love and garlic, used as the title of this chapter. Objects—garlic included—are relatively neutral topics of conversation; but love? Just try it, seriously. In the same way that an explanation of the punch line kills the joke, palaver about the apparently simplest aspects of human relations is likely to lead to more and more vexing problems. Of course, the best time for such "heart-to-heart" talks is late in the evening. By three o'clock in the morning even the simplest topic has been talked out beyond recognition and both partners are at the end of their endurance. A sleepless night is virtually guaranteed.

Further refinements of this technique involve a certain kind of question and a special category of demands. Here is an example of the former: Suppose your partner asks you, "Why are you angry at me?" Now, as far as you know, you are not angry at your partner or at anything else. But the question implies that the questioner knows better than you what goes on in your own mind, in other words, that the answer, "But I am not at all angry at you," is simply not true. This technique is also known as *mind reading* or *clairvoyance*, and it is so powerful because one can argue until doomsday about moods and their visible manifestations, and because most people become infuriated when negative feelings are attributed to them.

The other trick consists of person A confronting person B with allegations that, for best effect, should be both petulant and nebulous, as for example, "Today I remembered something about you that is very upsetting, but I decided to ignore it." If person B then wants to know what on earth A is talking about, A can snap the trap shut by explaining, "If you were not the kind of person you are, you would not have to ask. The mere fact that you don't even know what I mean shows your true nature." This technique has a venerable history, since it has been used for centuries and with great success in dealing with so-called mentally disturbed people. The way Rosencrantz and Guildenstern, at the behest of the King, attempt to find out what goes on in Hamlet's mind has some of this flavor. Whenever Hamlet notices their "looks which your modesties have not craft enough to colour" and wants to know what the two are up to, they resort to such lame replies as, "What should we say, my lord?" or, "To what end?"

or, "My lord, there was no such stuff in my thoughts."

To return to fact, consider what may happen when a so-called disturbed person demands unequivocally that his alleged madness be explained to him. This very question can be interpreted as further proof of his craziness: "If you were not upset, you would know what we are talking about." There is undeniable method in the madness of such a reply: As long as the so-called patient tacitly accepts the relationship definition, "We are normal, you are crazy," he admits that he is crazy; but when he questions it, his demand for clarification is itself turned into a sign of mental disturbance. After this unsuccessful excursion from his own world into the environment of other humans, he can either tear out his hair in helpless rage or fall back into his isolation. In either case he demonstrates even more clearly how disturbed he is and how right the others were from the beginning. The "effort to drive the other crazy" is a term coined by Harold F. Searles [21], but the technique was well known to Lewis Carroll. In *Through the Looking Glass* the Red and the White Queens accuse Alice of trying to deny something, and they ascribe this to her state of mind:

"I'm sure I didn't mean—" Alice was beginning, but the Red Queen interrupted her impatiently.

"That's just what I complain of! You should have meant! What do you suppose is the use of a child without any meaning? Even a joke should have a meaning—and a child is more important than a joke, I hope. You couldn't deny that, even if you tried with both hands."

"I don't deny things with my hands," Alice objected.

"Nobody said you did," said the Red Queen. "I said you couldn't if you tried."

"She is in that state of mind," said the White Queen, "that she wants to deny something—only she doesn't know what to deny!"

"A nasty, vicious temper," the Red Queen remarked; and then there was an uncomfortable silence for a minute or two.

In the establishments that consider themselves competent to treat such mental states, the applicability of this technique is limited only by the degree of one's inventiveness. For instance, it can be left up to the so-called patient to decide whether or not he wants to participate in certain ward activities. If he declines with thanks, he is requested, with earnest concern, to explain his reasons. What he then says is quite unimportant, for his explanation will in any case be a manifestation of his resistance to treatment and therefore pathological. The only alternative then open to him is participation in that particular therapeutic activity. However, he had better make sure not to let it slip out that he has no other choice, for to see his situation in these terms would still reveal his resistance and lack of insight. He must want to participate "spontaneously" (see Chapter 10), even though by participating he indirectly admits that he is sick and in need of treatment. In certain larger social systems that are fashioned after closed psychiatric wards, this technique is known by that disrespectful and reactionary term *brainwashing*. An extension of these remarks exceeds the scope of my modest manual. Let me return to my subject and summarize part of the foregoing.

A useful, effective way of complicating a relationship involves offering the partner two possibilities for his choice. As soon as he chooses one, he can be blamed for not having chosen the other. In the field of communication research this trick is called the Illusion of Alternatives, and it has a very simple structure. If the partner does A, he should have done B; but if he chooses B, he should be doing A. A particularly clear example can be found in Dan Greenburg's instructions to Jewish mothers already mentioned in the Introduction:

Give your son Marvin two sport shirts as a present. The first time he wears one of them, look at him sadly and say in your Basic Tone of Voice: "The other one you didn't like?" [4, p. 16]

But this trick also works the other way around. Most adolescents are naturally endowed experts in applying the illusion of alternatives.

Standing as they do in the no-man's-land between childhood and adulthood, they have little difficulty in demanding that their parents recognize them as young adults, with all the privileges and freedom of action implicit in adulthood. But when it comes to the duties and the responsibilities of adulthood, they can imply by word or action that they are much too young for these. And if their parents then grind their teeth and wish they had remained childless, teenagers can indignantly hold them up as people devoid of parental affection or concern. The teenagers win either way.

Psychiatrists and psychologists are still at a loss to explain why we all tend to get caught in an illusion of alternatives, while we usually find it much easier to reject either possibility if they are offered separately rather than together. In the pursuit of unhappiness we should utilize this empirical fact to the fullest if we wish to dedicate ourselves to the infernalization of our relationships. Here are three easy exercises for the beginner.

EXERCISE 1

Ask somebody to do something for you. As soon as he gets going, ask him for another favor. Since he can only satisfy your two requests successively and not simultaneously, victory is yours: If he wants to complete the first activity, you can complain that he is ignoring your second request, and vice versa. If he gets angry, you can sadly point out to him how moody he has been lately.

EXERCISE 2

Say or do something that another person could very well interpret either seriously or humorously. Depending on his reaction, you can now accuse him of either ridiculing a serious matter or having no sense of humor. (This example is borrowed from Searles' article mentioned earlier [21].)

EXERCISE 3

Ask your partner to read these last pages, claiming that they are a perfect description of his general attitude toward you. In the somewhat unlikely case of agreement, he has once and for all admitted the manipulative nature of his behavior toward you. If—and this is far more probable—he rejects your contention, you are still the winner. For you can now show him that with his rejection he has just done "it" again. Explain this by saying something like, "If I silently tolerate your manipulations, you manipulate me even more; if I point them out to

83

you, as I just did, you manipulate me by claiming that you don't manipulate me."

These are merely elementary examples. When you become a truly talented RDE, you can extend this technique into its full byzantine and labyrinthine complexity. Eventually your partner will have to ask himself seriously if he is not really crazy. At the very least, he will experience a vertiginous feeling in his head. Here, then, is a tactic that not only will allow you to prove your righteousness and normalcy, but also will supply a maximum of misery to both of you.

In addition, it is also useful to demand a hierarchy of assurances and to question each one on the next higher level as soon as you receive it. R. D. Laing's book *Do You Love Me?* [10] is relevant here; it contains masterful examples. In many of them the key word "really" plays a decisive role, as in the following exchange, which is not a direct quotation but which is meant to convey the flavor of this kind of conversation:

Do you love me?
Yes.
Really?
Yes, really.
Really really?

What follows are presumably "forest sounds," as Albee put it in *Who's Afraid of Vir-*

ginia Woolf?—screams, growls, and so forth. And as long as we are on this subject, here is one more useful suggestion.

As already mentioned in the Introduction to this book, it is difficult, if at all possible, to define happiness and contentment in positive terms. But this need not deter any paragon of virtue from ascribing a *negative* meaning to these concepts. As the reader probably knows, the unofficial motto of puritanism is, "You may do anything you want, as long as you don't enjoy it." And there are indeed people who consider it indecent to enjoy anything as long as our world is in its sorry state. Admittedly, it becomes difficult to enjoy even a drink of water while half a million innocent civilians are nearly dying of thirst in West Beirut. But even if general, worldwide happiness were to break out one of these days, a Calvinistic pessimist need not give up hope: He can always utilize Laing's recipe by reproaching his innocently happy partner with, "How dare you have fun when Christ died on the Cross for you! Was He having fun?" [9, p. 2]. The rest is embarrassed silence.

Chapter Ten

"Be Spontaneous!"

So far we have been concerned with a number of variations on the basic theme of "love or garlic." But these are relatively harmless skirmishes compared to the explosive power of the seemingly innocent demand for spontaneous behavior. Of all the knots, tangles, and other booby traps in the arsenal of an experienced RDE, the "Be spontaneous!" paradox is by far the most universally utilized. And a real, kosher paradox it is, satisfying even the most stringent requirements of formal logic.

In the pristine halls of logical Olympus, coercion and spontaneity (i.e., that which proceeds from within without constraint and external force) are incompatible. To do spontaneously what one has been commanded to do is just as impossible as to forget by an act of conscious decision or to deliberately sleep more deeply. Either we act spontaneously, that is, at our own discretion, or we comply with a command and therefore do not act spontaneously. From a purely logical point of view we cannot do both at the same time.

But so what? What do we care about logic? Just as I can write, "Be spontaneous!" I can also say it—logic or no logic. Paper and sound waves are patient. The recipient of such a message is probably a little less patient. For what can he now do?

If you have read John Fowles' novel *The Collector*, you know what I am trying to get at. The collector is a young man who at first limits himself to butterflies whose beauty he can admire at leisure and safely. After all, they are impaled on pins and cannot fly away. But when he falls in love with the beautiful student Miranda and tries to use the same technique with her (following the formula "more of the same," mentioned on p. 31), he quickly gets himself (and her) into trouble. As the young man is not especially handsome and does not think too highly of himself, he is forced to assume that Miranda will not fall in love with him spontaneously. He therefore abducts her and instead of pins utilizes a lonely cottage to keep her his prisoner. Within the frame of this naked coercion, he seriously hopes and expects that she will gradually come to like him. Needless to say, for her this captivity becomes an ever increasing nightmare. Only very gradually does the inexorable and hopeless tragedy of his "Be spontaneous!" paradox dawn upon the young man and he realizes how he has made impossible precisely that which he wanted to achieve. Worse yet, he cannot simply call it a mistake and let Miranda go, because he would be arrested for a very serious crime.

Farfetched? Too "literary"? All right, take this far more trivial situation whose production does not require any particular deviousness. It is the hackneyed example of the mother who demands that her little son do his homework— not just because it is a school requirement, but because he should *like* doing it. What we discover here is the reversal of the definition of puritanism mentioned earlier. Instead of, "It is your duty not to have fun," the basic rule here is, "Your duty should be fun."

What is one to do? The question, here repeated, is rhetorical, for there is no solution. What is the wife to do whose husband not only demands that she make herself available to him sexually whenever he feels like it, but asks that she fully enjoy it every time? What can one do if one is in the shoes of that boy who should *like* to do his homework? One either assumes that there is something wrong with oneself or with the world. But since there is very little one can do about "the world," one is virtually forced to look for the blame within oneself. This does not sound very convincing, does it? Please read on; it is simpler than you may think.

Suppose you were born into a family in which—for whatever reason—everybody is supposed to be happy. Or, to put it more precisely, a family in which the parents subscribe to the idea that a child's sunny disposition is the best proof of parental success. And now see what happens when you are in a bad mood, or tired, or afraid of your physical education class, the dentist, or the dark, or if you do not want to become a Boy Scout. Your parents will not see this as a temporary mood, a passing state of fatigue and crankiness, a typical childhood anxiety, or the like. For them it will be a silent but all the more outspoken accusation of parental failure. And against this accusation they will defend themselves by reminding you what and how much they have done for you, what sacrifices they had to make, and how little right and reason you have not to be happy.

Some parents can push this technique to

masterful perfection, telling the child, for instance, something like, "Go to your room and don't come out until you have a smile on your face." In saying this they are implying something very clearly without spelling it out, namely, that with a little effort and goodwill the child should be able to reprogram his feelings from bad to good. All he has to do is innervate the correct facial muscles to produce that smile which will reestablish his citizenship as a "good" person in the world of all "good" people.

This simple recipe whereby sadness and moral inferiority—and especially ingratitude—can be thrown into the same stew as garlic and love is of considerable importance to the pursuit of unhappiness. It is guaranteed to plunge the other person into deep guilt feelings, which, in turn, can then be defined as part of those feelings he would not have if he were not the kind of person he is. And if he has the cheek to ask how on earth he is supposed to reset the dials of his feelings, it can be pointed out to him that this, too, is something that a good person can accomplish and does not have to be told. (At this point don't forget to raise your eyebrows and look sad.)

Once a person's sadness training has progressed sufficiently, he should be able to generate his depressions all by himself. But this degree of proficiency has to be reached first, for it is virtually impossible to produce these guilt feelings in untrained people. I have in mind those thick-headed and unimaginative types who have temporary bad moods, just as the depression candidates do, but who hold the simplistic view that occasional sadness is part and parcel of every life. For them, for whatever reason, sadness comes and goes, and if it is not over by tonight, it will be gone by tomorrow morning. No, depression is something else. It is the ability to continue telling oneself what one was told in childhood, namely, that one has neither right nor reason to be sad. The person who does this assiduously may rest assured that the depression will become deeper and last longer.

Family and friends who, following the dictates of common sense and their guileless hearts, try to come to the rescue of the depressed person by cheering him up and encouraging him to pull himself together will be naïvely astonished to find that it "somehow" makes things worse. For now the victim can feel doubly guilty; he should not only not be depressed, but he can also accuse himself of being unable to share in the rosy outlook of those kind people and of having bitterly disappointed their good intentions. Hamlet, for instance, was quite aware of the painful difference between his view of the world and that of others, but we must admiringly concede that he succeeded in making the most of it for his own purposes:

> I have of late—but wherefore I know not—lost all my mirth, foregone all custom of exercise; and indeed it goes so heavily with my disposition that this goodly frame, the earth, seems to me a sterile promontory, this most excellent canopy, the air, look you, this brave o'erhanging firmament, this majestical roof fretted with golden fire, why, it appears no other thing to me than a foul and pestilent congregation of vapours. What a piece of work is man! How noble in reason! How infinite in faculty, in form and moving! How express and admirable in action! How like an angel in apprehension! How like a god! The beauty of the world! The paragon of animals! And yet, to me, what is this quintessence of dust? Man delights not me. . . .

It does not seem to make much difference whether we prescribe the "Be happy!" paradox for ourselves or whether it is imposed on us by some outside authority. Furthermore, "Be happy" is only one of the many variations on the basic theme of "Be spontaneous!" Virtually *any* spontaneous behavior lends itself to the construction of inescapable traps: the demand for spontaneous remembering or forgetting; the wish for a particular gift and the disappointment when one receives it "only" because one stated that wish; the attempt to will an erection or an orgasm, which makes impossible precisely that which it was supposed to achieve; the resolve to fall asleep because one wants to sleep; or the demand for love as a moral obligation that leads to the impossibility of loving.

Chapter Eleven

Why Would Anybody Love Me?

LOVE, of course, is an inexhaustible subject. Therefore I shall not attempt to do more than dissect a very few of its most misery-producing aspects. To this end, I should first remind you of Dostoyevsky's intriguing suggestion that the biblical injunction to "love thy neighbor as thyself" makes more sense if it is turned upside-down, that is, one can love one's neighbor only if one loves *oneself*.

Less elegantly, but more to the point, the same idea was expressed decades later by Marx (Groucho, that is, not Karl): "I would not dream of belonging to a club that is willing to have me as a member." If you can fathom the depth of this *bon mot,* you are already well prepared for what is to follow.

To be loved is a mysterious thing, even under the best of circumstances. And it does not help much to try and inquire about love; if anything, asking about it muddles the situation further. At best, the other person cannot tell you why he loves you; at worst, his reason for loving you turns out to be something about yourself you have never thought to be particularly lovable—for instance, the mole on your left shoulder. Once more we realize that silence is golden.

So here is another useful lesson for the pursuit of our subject: Do not simply and gratefully accept what life offers you by way of your partner's affection. Ponder. Ask yourself—but not him—why he is fond of you. For he must have a vested interest or some other selfish reason that he is not likely to reveal to you.

Love is a paradox that has puzzled minds greater than yours and mine. It is the source from which some of the most celebrated creations of world literature have drawn their inspiration. Consider the following sentence from one of Rousseau's letters to Madame d'Houdetot: "If you are mine, I lose, though possessing you, her whom I honour" [17]. Reading this sentence twice may help. For what Rousseau appears to be saying is a bit startling for the average consumer: If you, my beloved, yield to me, then, by this very fact, you are no longer suitable to be the personification of my love. This exalted, eighteenth century view of love is still alive and well in our day, especially in a certain Mediterranean country where the male, having convinced himself of the fiery nature of his love, implores and assails the lady of his choice. When she eventually accedes to his petulance, he promptly despises her; a decent woman would never have yielded. Not surprisingly, that same country is also known to have the rule (whose existence is, of course, officially denied), "All women are whores, except my mother—she was a saint." (Naturally, she would not allow "it.")

In *Being and Nothingness*, Jean-Paul Sartre defines love as the vain attempt to possess freedom as freedom. He writes,

The lover cannot be satisfied with that superior form of freedom which is a free and voluntary engagement. Who would be content with a love given as pure loyalty to a sworn oath? Who would be satisfied with the words, "I love you because I freely engaged myself to love you and because I do not wish to go back on my word." Thus the lover demands a pledge, yet is irritated by a pledge. He wants to be loved by a freedom but demands that this freedom as freedom should no longer be free [20, pp. 478–479].

For the reader who wants to know more about these untenable and yet inescapable complications of love (and of many other forms of irrational behavior), the book *Ulysses and the Sirens* [1] by the Norwegian philosopher Jon Elster will afford unusual and fascinating reading. For the beginner, however, what has been said so far should provide a reliable point of departure. While he may not be able to achieve the expertise of the Groucho Marxes of this world, he need not relegate himself permanently to a low level of proficiency. The key requirement is merely a disbelief in his own lovability. On the strength of this fundamental conviction he can casually discredit anybody who loves him, for there is evidently something wrong with a person who loves somebody who is unworthy of love. A character defect like masochism, a neurotic dependence on a castrating mother, a morbid fascination with inferiority—all are possible reasons that offer themselves as clinical explanations for that person's misplaced love, making it uninteresting or even unsufferable. (A certain knowledge of psychology or at least some experience with encounter groups will greatly facilitate the choice of an appropriate diagnosis.)

Once such a diagnosis has been found, the shabbiness of the lover, of the beloved, and of love itself will be revealed. What more can one hope for? In his book *Knots*, Ronald Laing gives us a blueprint for this dilemma that is the best I know:

I don't respect myself
I can't respect anyone who respects me.
I can only respect someone who does not respect me.
I respect Jack
because he does not respect me
I despise Tom
because he does not despise me
Only a despicable person
can respect someone as despicable as me
I cannot love someone I despise
Since I love Jack
I cannot believe he loves me
What proof can he give?   [9, p. 18]

At first blush this may seem absurd, for the complications produced by this view of oneself and the other are so patently obvious. But this need not deter us or otherwise keep us out of misery, for, as Shakespeare so wisely put it in one of his sonnets,

All this the world well knows; yet none knows well
To shun the heaven that leads man to this hell.

And once you are safely in this hell, the rest is easy: Become enamored in a totally hopeless fashion with a married partner, priest, film star, or opera singer. In this way you will travel hopefully without ever arriving, and you will be spared the sobering discovery that an uncommitted, available person may be perfectly willing to enter into a relationship with you—at which point that person will immediately become despicable to you.

Chapter Twelve

The Traps of Helping

WHO loves is willing to help the beloved. But the spontaneous wish to help a human being does not necessarily presuppose that the person is close. In fact, the willingness to help a *stranger* is considered particularly noble. Unselfish help is a lofty ideal and (allegedly) contains its own reward.

This need not become an obstacle to our pursuit. Like any other noble attitude, the willingness to help can be tainted by the pale cast of thought. In order to doubt the unselfishness and purity of our gesture, we merely ask ourselves if we do not, after all, have a hidden agenda. Did I do my good deed as a deposit in my savings account in heaven? To impress other people? To be admired? To force somebody to be grateful to me? Or simply in order to alleviate some guilt feelings? Obviously there are no limits to the power of negative thinking, and he who seeks shall find. To the pure, everything is pure; the pessimist, on the other hand, will succeed in finding the cloven hoof, the Achilles heel, or whatever other metaphors there are in the field of podiatry.

If this seems difficult, consult the pertinent professional literature. It will open your eyes. You will discover that deep down the brave fireman is really a pyromaniac; the heroic soldier acts out his suicidal tendencies or, as the case may be, his murderous impulses; policemen delve into other people's crimes in order to resist becoming delinquents themselves; the famous detective barely manages to socialize his paranoid personality trends; every surgeon is really a secret sadist; the gynecologist is a voyeur; and the psychiatrist wants to play God. Voilà—it's that easy to unmask the basic rottenness of the world.

But even those helpers who fail to discover and appreciate these real motivations can turn helping into a special hell, a hell that may be quite beyond the imagination of the uneducated layman. All that is required is a relationship based predominantly on the fact that one partner needs (or claims to need) help, while the other supplies it. It is in the nature of such a relationship that it can only have one of two possible outcomes, and both are fatal: Either the helping gets nowhere, or it succeeds. Once again, *tertium non datur*, as the old Romans put it—there is no third possibility. In the first case, even the most inveterate helper will eventually have enough and will withdraw from the relationship. But if the helper has success, it follows that the other no longer needs help, and the relationship will fall apart because it has lost its meaning. (I know, I know—the idealists among my readers will say, "And now the two can establish a mature, totally new relationship." Try and sell this idea to a real helper!)

From a literary point of view, we are immediately reminded of the numerous eighteenth and nineteenth century novels and libretti in which a young nobleman devotes his life to the salvation of the wanton, demoniacal (but in her heart of hearts innocent and lovable) prostitute. More practical examples are provided by the nearly always intelligent, responsible, self-sacrificing women who are animated by a fatal temptation to redeem alcoholics, gamblers, or delinquents through the gentle power of their love, who until the bitter end will react to the unchanging behavior of the man with more of the same devotion and helpfulness. With regard to misery potential, these relationships are almost perfect, for the two partners complement each other to a point that is virtually impossible under more positive circumstances. In order to sacrifice herself, such a woman needs a problem-ridden, weak man, for in the life of a reasonably functioning and independent partner there is, as she sees it, neither enough room nor need for her love and thus for herself. He, on the other hand, needs an undaunted helper who permits him to continue his long series of failures. A female who subscribes to the principle that one hand washes the other is likely to get out of such a relationship very quickly—if she gets into it in the first place. Thus our recipe is: Find a partner who through her being the way she is enables you to be the way you want to be, but, here too, beware of arriving!

In communication theory this pattern is known by the term *collusion*. It refers to a subtle arrangement, a *quid pro quo*, an (often unconscious) arrangement on the relationship level in which I let myself be confirmed and ratified by my partner in the way I see myself and want to be seen. The uninitiated beginner may naïvely ask why one needs a partner. The answer is simple: Imagine a mother without a child, a doctor without patients, a chief of state without a state. These people would be shadows, provisional humans, so to speak. Only a partner who plays the correct, required role in relation to us can make us "real"; without him or her we would have to rely on our dreams and they are known to be unreal. But why should anybody be willing to play this specific role for me? There are two possible reasons:

1. The role he *must* play in order to make me feel "real" is the very role he *wants* to play in order to bring about his own "reality." The first impression is that of a perfect fit, isn't it? This being so, it would seem to be totally useless for our purposes. But notice, please, that in order to remain perfect, the relation must not undergo the slightest change. Nevertheless, time goes on; children have the unfortunate tendency to grow up; patients tend to get well; and the original elation is soon followed by disillusionment and the desperate attempt to prevent the other from escaping the increasingly intolerable bind. Let me quote Sartre again.

While I attempt to free myself from the hold of the Other, the Other is trying to free himself from mine; while I seek to enslave the Other, the Other seeks to enslave me. We are by no means dealing with unilateral relations with an object-in-itself, but with reciprocal and moving relations [20, pp. 474–475].

Since any collusion presupposes that the other must, on his own terms, be exactly the way

I want him to be, the result is an unavoidable "Be spontaneous!" paradox.

2. The fatality of this outcome becomes even more obvious when we examine the second reason why a partner may be willing to play the complementary role from which the sense of being "real" is derived. This involves adequate compensation for the services rendered. The example of prostitution immediately comes to mind. The client wants the female to surrender to him not just for money, but because she "really" wants to. (Notice how this wondrous concept of "really" keeps popping up.) Not surprisingly, only a truly gifted courtesan manages to awaken and maintain this illusion. With less talented practitioners this is exactly the point at which the client's disillusionment sets in. But our examination must not be limited to prostitution in the narrow sense of the term; disillusionment is likely to arise whenever collusive expectations or demands invade a relationship. As the saying goes, a sadist is somebody who is nice to a masochist. The problem of many homosexual relations is due to the hope for closeness with a "real" man, while the other invariably turns out to be either a homosexual himself or not interested in the relationship.

In his play *The Balcony*, Jean Genet sketches a vivid picture of such a collusive world. In

Madame Irma's superbrothel, the prostitutes not only cater to their clients' sexual fantasies, but perform—for a fee, of course—*any* complementary role that a client may need in order to act out his dream. At one point Madame Irma enumerates her clients: two kings of France, with coronation ceremonies and different rituals; an admiral on the bridge of his sinking ship; a bishop in a state of perpetual adoration; a judge trying a thief; a general on horseback; and many others. (And all this while the revolution is raging and the northern half of the city is already lost to the rebels.) Even Madame Irma's excellent organization cannot totally prevent disappointing letdowns. As can be imagined, the clients find it difficult to forget (be it spontaneously or deliberately) that they are paying for the charade. A further sobering nuisance is the fact that the hired partners either cannot, or do not care to, play their roles exactly as the clients want them to be played in order to create the hoped-for "reality." Take, for instance, the following dialogue between the "judge" and the "thief":

> THE JUDGE: My being a judge is an emanation of your being a thief. You need only refuse—but you'd better not!—need only refuse to be who you

are—what you are, therefore who you are—for me to cease to be . . . to vanish, evaporated. Burst. Volatized. Denied. . . . . What then? What then? But you won't refuse, will you? You won't refuse to be a thief? That would be wicked. That would be criminal. You'd deprive me of being! (*Imploringly*) Say it, my child, my love, you won't refuse?

THE THIEF (*coyly*): I might.

THE JUDGE: What's that? What's that you say? You'd refuse? Tell me where. And tell me again what you have stolen.

THE THIEF (*curtly, and getting up*): I won't.

THE JUDGE: Tell me where. Don't be cruel. . . .

THE THIEF: Your tone is getting too familiar. I won't have it!

THE JUDGE: Miss. . . . Madame. I beg of you. (*He falls to his knees.*) Look, I beseech you. Don't leave me in this position, waiting to be a judge. If there were no judges, what would become of us, but if there were no thieves? [3, pp. 14–15]

The play ends with Madame Irma addressing the audience at the end of her hard day's night: "You must now go home, where everything—you can be quite sure—will be even falser than here." She turns out the last lights. There is a burst of machine-gun fire, threateningly close.

Chapter Thirteen

Those Crazy Foreigners

LIKE most bitter truths, Madame Irma's last remark is unlikely to earn her much sympathy. We do not like to be reminded of the mendacity of our private world. For our world is supposed to be the true world; it is the other world or, rather, the worlds of the others that are crazy, deceptive, illusory, and weird. And from this we can learn a lot that is useful for the pursuit of unhappiness.

I do not intend (nor would I be competent) to contribute wise words to the debate about why there are tensions between the citizens of a country and their ethnic minorities. The problem is universal: with Mexicans, Vietnamese, or Haitians in the United States; North Africans in France; East Indians in Africa; Italians in Switzerland; Turks in West Germany; to say nothing of the problems found by Armenians, Kurds, Druzes, Shiites, and others. A complete list would be very long indeed.

In order to get all worked up about foreigners we need no more than a few personal contacts or even indirect observations, whether in our home country or abroad. Belching during and after a meal once was a compliment to the host; nowadays it does not have this meaning. But do you know that occasional smacking of the lips and audible sucking of air through the teeth during a meal still has a polite connotation for the Japanese? Or that you can make yourself extremely unpopular in Central America if you indicate the height of a person by the "obvious" gesture, namely, with the hand held out horizontally? Only the height of animals may be indicated in this way.

And speaking of Latin America, you are probably aware of or at least have heard of that epitome of masculinity, the Latin Lover. Basically he is a lovable, harmless character, and his social role suits the wider societal contexts of Latin American cultures, which even now are fairly strict. What I mean is that there still are— at least officially—strict limits to romantic, premarital escapades in so-called proper society. This allows the Latin Lover to engage in that passionately languishing behavior that is the perfect complement to the sensual, smoldering, but totally unyielding attitude of the beautiful *Latinas*. Small wonder, then, that Latin American folk songs (above all the nostalgically beautiful *boleros*) never cease to exalt the pangs of unrequited, unattainable love, the fateful separation just before the ultimate fulfillment, or the tear-choked splendor of the *última noche*, the first and irrevocably last night. But after listening to a larger number of these songs, the less romantically minded foreigner begins to wonder if that is all there is to it. Making allowance for the occasional exception, the answer is *yes*.

Let us now export the Latin Lover to the United States or Scandinavia, and a horde of problems results. Our lover will continue to assail the local beauties with his adoring routines; the game as played by American and Scandinavian women is based on very different rules, however, and these beauties are likely to take him seriously. But this is something that he expects as little as you or I expect to inherit a big fortune—pleasant as the fantasy is in and of itself. By the rules of *his* game they have to reject him or put him off until the wedding night. It is not too difficult to imagine the disappointing complications for the eager women and the threat to the Latin Lover's capabilities, which so far have only had to pass the test of the *última noche*. Again we appreciate how much better it is to travel hopefully than to arrive.

Similar problems now beset Italian males thanks to the gradual emancipation of their female counterparts. Formerly the Italian male could behave as passionately as he considered himself obligated to. The risk was small, for the female in question would almost reliably oppose his advances. One of the basic rules of male behavior was: If I am alone with a woman, any woman, for more than five minutes and do not try to touch her, she will think that I am a homosexual. The problem now is that the women are far more open-minded, and to the extent that psychiatric statistics may be believed, the number of men who are being treated for impotence has greatly increased. To perform the fiery male routine is safe only as long as the partner can be trusted to adopt the "right" complementary attitude and reject advances in a coy but motherly fashion.

Europeans who travel to the United States are likely to find themselves in a predicament that is the direct opposite of that of the Latin Lover. There exists in every culture a certain brief time during which one may have direct eye contact with a stranger. When this time span is exceeded, even if only by a second, the results in Europe and those in the United States are very different. In Europe the other person usually becomes annoyed or even suspicious and looks away; in North America, however, he (and especially she) smiles. This totally unexpected reaction may lead even the most timid European to assume special sympathies in the other—love at first sight, so to speak—and to anticipate that the situation offers unexpected opportunities. It does not offer them at all; the rules of the game are different.

Why this hodgepodge of pseudo-ethnic oddities? Not simply to impress you with my cosmopolitan knowledge, dear reader, but to enable you to turn your foreign travels (or the visit of foreigners to your office or home) into a reliable disappointment. Again the principle is quite elementary: In the face of all evidence to the contrary, assume that your own behavior is obvious and normal under any and all circumstances. As soon as you do this, any different behavior in the same situation will appear crazy or at least silly.

Chapter Fourteen

Life as a Game

THE psychologist Alan Watts once said that life is a game where Rule No. 1 is: This is no game, this is serious. And Laing must have had something similar in mind when, in *Knots*, he wrote, "They are playing a game. They are playing at not playing a game" [9, p. 1].

We have seen, more than once, that a fundamental precondition for the attainment of misery is the ability not to let our right hand know what the left is doing. In this way we can play Watts' or Laing's game with ourselves.

These are not idle fantasies. There is even a branch of higher mathematics, namely game theory, that has been dealing with these and related problems since the 1920s. And from this domain we want to draw our last inspiration. Of course, for the mathematician the term *game* has no childish or playful meaning. Rather, for him it is the name of a conceptual frame that is governed by a body of specific rules which, in turn, determine the possible behaviors of the participants (the players). It goes without saying that one's chances of winning are enhanced by the understanding and optimal application of these rules.

Game theory makes a fundamental distinction between two types of games, namely, zero-sum and non-zero-sum games. Let us look first at zero-sum games. These are the ones in which the loss of one player constitutes the gain of the other. In other words, gains and losses, added together, always amount to zero. Every simple bet between two persons is based on this basic principle—what I lose, you win. (There can, of course, be far more complicated zero-sum games than this, but the principle remains the same.)

Non-zero-sum games, on the other hand, are those in which, as the name implies, losses and gains do not cancel each other out. This means that their sum may lie above or below zero; in this kind of game both players (or if more than two are involved, *all* players) may win or lose. This may seem puzzling at first, but examples readily come to mind, a strike, for instance. Generally during a strike *both* players—management and work force—lose. For even if an advantage should materialize for one side or the other in the course of the dispute, the overall sum of gains and losses does not necessarily add up to zero, but may be a negative number.

Now let us imagine that the loss of production resulting from the strike turns out to be a boon for a competitor, who can now sell a lot more of his products than before. On this level, then, the situation may very well have the characteristics of a zero-sum game: The losses of the firm on strike may be equal to the additional profits of the competitor. But note that the first firm's losses are inflicted on both management *and* workers, and in this sense they *both* become losers.

Descending now from the abstract realm of mathematics and collective skirmishes to the level of interpersonal relations, the following question arises: Is human partnership a zero-sum or a non-zero-sum game? To answer this question we shall have to find out whether the "gains" of one partner can be considered the "losses" of the other.

And on this point opinions are likely to differ widely. If the problem were merely a question of who is objectively right (on the object level) and who, therefore, is wrong in a given situation, that could be a zero-sum game. This is what many relationships are mostly about. To get into this hell it is quite sufficient for one partner to see life in general as a zero-sum game, offering *only* the alternative between victory and defeat. From then on, everything else follows with ease. Even if the other did not originally see life as a constant street fight, he can be converted to this view. The first partner only needs to insist on playing a zero-sum game on the relationship level, and one may rest assured that things will go to hell. For what zero-sum players are likely to overlook, stuck as they are with the idea of having to win so as not to lose, is that greatest opponent of all, life, and all that life has to offer quite apart from victory and defeat. *Vis-à-vis* that opponent, both zero-sum partners lose.

Why is it so difficult for us to realize that life is a non-zero-sum game? That we can *both* win so long as we are not obsessed with the need to defeat the partner so as not to be defeated by him? And why is it totally impossible for the expert zero-sum players among us to imagine that we can live in harmony with that all-embracing partner life?

These are rhetorical questions, the very ones that Friedrich Nietzsche addressed in *Beyond Good and Evil* when he claimed that madness in individuals is rare, but in groups, nations, and epochs it is the rule. Why should we average mortals be any wiser than politicians, ideologists, and even the superpowers? Always use the big stick, or, as Kaiser Wilhelm used to say, *"viel Feind, viel Ehr'*," many enemies, much honor.

The only rule that could terminate this game is not itself one of the rules of the game. It comes in different guises, but they all add up to the same thing, and they involve such qualities as fairness, tolerance, and trust. Without them, the game becomes a game without end.

Intellectually we have always known about this rule. (There is even an obscure proverb to the effect that life gives us what we are willing to put into it: As the question, so voice the answer.) On the gut level, however, only a few truly happy people believe it. For if we could believe it, we would know that we are not only the creators of our misery, but can just as well construct our happiness.

This little book began with a passage from Dostoyevsky, and perhaps it should conclude with another quotation from his work. In *The Possessed,* one of Dostoyevsky's most enigmatic characters has this to say:

Everything's good . . . . Everything. Man is unhappy because he doesn't know he is happy. It's only that. That's all, that's all! If one finds out, one will become happy at once, that minute.

The situation is hopeless and the solution hopelessly simple.

Bibliography

1. Elster, Jon. *Ulysses and the Sirens: Studies in Rationality and Irrationality.* Cambridge University Press, Cambridge, and Editions de la Maison des Sciences de l'Homme, Paris, 1979.
2. Fairlie, Henry. "My Favorite Sociologist." *The New Republic,* 7 October 1978, p. 43.
3. Genet, Jean. *The Balcony* (translated by Bernard Frechtman). Grove Press, New York, 1966.
4. Greenburg, Dan. *How to Be a Jewish Mother.* Price/Stern/Sloane, Los Angeles, 1964.
5. Greenburg, Dan. *How to Make Yourself Miserable.* Random House, New York, 1966.
6. Gulotta, Guglielmo. *Commedie e drammi nel matrimonio.* Feltrinelli, Milan, 1976.

7. Keesee, Bobby J. Quoted in *The San Francisco Chronicle*, 29 April 1975, p. 15.
8. Kubie, Lawrence S. "The destructive potential in humor." *American Journal of Psychiatry* 127, 1971, 861–866.
9. Laing, Ronald D. *Knots*. Pantheon Books, New York, 1970.
10. Laing, Ronald D. *Do You Love Me?* Pantheon Books, New York, 1976, p. 86.
11. Maryn, Mike. Quoted in *The San Francisco Chronicle*, 28 July 1977, p. 1.
12. Morisette, Rodolphe and Luc. *Petit manuel de guérilla matrimoniale*. Ferron, Montreal, 1973.
13. Orwell, George. "Revenge is sour." In *The Collected Essays, Journalism and Letters of George Orwell* (Sonia Orwell and Ian Angus, eds.). Harcourt, Brace & World, New York, 1968, Vol. 4, pp. 3–6.
14. Parkinson, Cyril N. *Parkinson's Law and Other Studies in Administration*. Houghton Mifflin, Boston, 1957.
15. Parkinson, Cyril N. *Mrs. Parkinson's Law and Other Studies in Domestic Science*. Houghton Mifflin, Boston, 1968.
16. Peter, Laurence J. *The Peter Principle*. Morrow, New York, 1969.
17. Peyre, H. *Literature and Sincerity*. Yale University Press, New Haven, Connecticut, 1963, quoted on p. 93.
18. Potter, Stephen. *The Complete Upmanship*. Holt, Rinehart & Winston, New York, 1971.
19. Ross, Nancy W. (ed.). "The subjugation of a

ghost." In *The World of Zen.* Random House, New York, 1960, p. 82.

20. Sartre Jean-Paul. *Being and Nothingness* (translated by Hazel E. Barnes). Washington Square Press, New York, 1966.

21. Searles, Harold F. "The effort to drive the other person crazy—An element in the aetiology and psychotherapy of schizophrenia." *British Journal of Medical Psychology* 32, 1959, 1–18.

22. Selvini Palazzoli, Mara, et al. *Il Mago smagato.* Feltrinelli Economica, Milan, 1976.

23. Spaemann, Robert. "Philosophie als Lehre vom glücklichen Leben." *Neue Zürcher Zeitung* 260, 1977, 66.

24. U.S. Bureau of Census. *Statistical Abstracts of the United States,* 102nd ed. Washington, D.C., 1981.